We Do
do ESP

JOHN BROWNE

Ordering Information:

Prime Seven Media
518 Landmann St.
Tomah City, WI 54660

Printed in the United States of America

TABLE OF CONTENTS

CHAPTER 1

SMELL

*F*or years I have picked up on smells not associated with my surroundings or of my own making, how did this come about? God seems to have reminded us that he gave us these senses and can add or take them away, due to the fact that I was unsure of why we were given each other's senses as well as our own only God knows.

I one day was very aware of a strong smell of gas, this was not a normal situation i.e. it wasn't the fact I smelt gas but the circumstances why this was brought to my attention, it was not in my vicinity but in a different place many miles away and coming from another person's nose, Louise, this was explained to me as not something she would do herself but she was forced to put her head into a gas oven and breathe in the gas. I at first thought that she was trying to commit suicide but found out it was really due to force of 4 callous types that have invaded her life like the plague they really are.

Louise and I at this point had been secretly talking for 3 years previous as I have been listening to the 4 and their slating of me and my music making prowess, it developed into a mockery every day as I produced music she would be told off as she was following my progress and due to the fact that they had been hooked up with monitoring facilities which are audio as well as visual. This form of monitoring is not only illegal but has been provided by the owners of her flat and is not acceptable at all.

She at the moment has to go through having solid waste smeared on her person every day, I smell the shit when it has been applied to her person thru her own nose.

The 4 (Male) smell absolutely disgusting due to not having washed for 15 years as you can tell there must be a build-up of body odour and due to the fact they rub faeces over Louise using their hands, they must be in a very sorry state, they also eat faeces on a regular basis and although it seems so have not as yet visited her majesties pleasure, known as an old prison trait for those forced to do it, these 4 do it with gusto and pleasure all in front of Louise which is how I manage to smell their goings on and with the verbal help of Louise explaining what is going at that particular time.

The 4 are gay and don't want to come out of the closet, but commit gay acts in front of her, which both she and I do not agree with being Christians, they do not wash at all so the smegma is overpowering and an insult to both Louise, God & myself but is one of the main reasons they do it, committing oral sex on each other, licking very unclean bottoms, using fingers and tongues to remove excess faeces from each other as they do their disgusting thing again in front of her.

They have lately been lifting their arms to force Louise to breathe in their B O to insult both her and I as they have had all explained about our E.S.P. and that it includes smell.

CHAPTER 2

WEAPONS

The 4 have 2 knives each, a sword each, a retractable double edged pole possibly 4 to 5 feet in length when extended. They also have knives with a hook to them and scalpels which all have been used on Louise over a 15 year period to date (15/05/13) also having firearms consisting of 2 pistols each with 2 of them have a rifle with a pistol each. They also have countless rounds of ammunition which they have bragged about.

They have an oxy acetylene torch modified to use petrol each which they use with gusto for administrating torture on Louise, burning her daytime and sometimes throughout the night while she is trying to sleep.

They have a bottle or few bottles of chloroform each and use this on her every day and night to send her to sleep while they administer torture via fire, cold/hot water, soapy water on her wounds and in her eyes.

How they use their weapons has been a crime from day one, put simply all 4 use them on Louise all day and most of the night, WHY? Due to the fact that the owners of her flat have given consent to, they have also given them Cocaine which they use to stay in the torturous mood and to stay up due to paranoia. The 4 have been given in payment copious amounts of cocaine i.e. enough to last all 4 of them several years. They have also tried to force feed Louise with cocaine and due to the fact that she hates it along with myself, this has only made them try harder.

All of the knives that were in her kitchen have been moved to the second bedroom so this would not get in the way of their torturing techniques because that way Louise would be able to fight back and due to their way they have encouraged her to fight back without the use of any weapons, all heavy items that could be used as a weapon have also been place in the second bedroom and locked so there is no way of Louise being allowed to really fight back, the key is with one of the 4 along with her debit card, keys to her front door and her purse/wallet.

They have burnt her with the torches, boiling hot water, used cold water to soak her from head to toe, used petrol to coat her in threatening to ignite the petrol if she didn't do what she was told or in their case just for a laugh. They have deployed this type of torture many, many, times and don't let up as the keep working in ever decreasing circles and eventually come back to what they have done before.

They cut and stab her in every part of the body including her face, stomach, vagina, bottom, back they have removed the hard bit of the chair back leaving only the material to lean on so they can administer their evil traits, neck which they have threatened to kill her using this method via her throat of which they have practised every time I smoke a cigarette they cut her across the throat normally on every drag of the cigarette. They cut and stab her legs, feet, toes, the soles of her feet. They are at the moment working on the kidney area and with gusto. Also her hands while we are typing and her fingers, the wrists have been cut on a number of occasions. They say that when she is found people will believe that she is a self harmer, she is not!

CHAPTER 3

THE RAPES

The owners of the flat have already attacked Louise to make sure she is intimidated and scarred as well as scared for life with the threats of the situation being made worse when they return to her flat; these are the couple along with their minions that have already raped Louise threatening to do worse. They allegedly are also paedophiles along with the 4 having bragged about the children they have rapped already and the 4 have been promised if they carry out their duties they will be allowed to rape again, at the moment they have become impotent which encourages them to act out their gay acts in front of Louise all the more as they say they are trying to get their mojo back. The 4 when they raped her had to be explained to me afterwards, being a man it is not a feeling I would recommend and feel for Louise have undergone this type of treatment from the 4's Hierarchy as they call themselves or the 4 who if they weren't made (we feel by god) impotent would have insisted on carrying out more rapes on Louise and insist on being allowed to try again, she has spurned their wishes and is being tortured more for having the nerve to say NO!

The 4 have bragged about having rapped minimum of 2 children each with 2 having raped at least 3 kids each. They all come from Manchester and have escaped to London where Louise resides. One of the 4 raped his own child and also his wife, they come from Solihull allegedly. They have worked in schools allegedly in and around, but as these were explained to Louise by them we both take the bragging as true due to the nature of the beast, they all worship the devil and have explained a crazy plan to try to hoodwink God into believing they are Christians and kidnapping God and taking him to the devil to answer to the devil for casting him out of heaven. This is the warped mind of the 4 lunatics we are dealing with today.

They have threatened to rape me and continue their torture on me when they get the chance to move in on me either by breaking into my house and waiting for me to return from a journey or while I am in my house and blowing out the electricity, the front or back door, entering and continue with their crazy goings on with me for the rest of my life. They have also threatened my children and brothers and sisters to try to get me to comply to their wishes. They have said they want to move in so they can learn of E.S.P. which is a farce.

When they rapped Louise and from since then they have been able to track our conversations in Telepathy and physcokenisis i.e. verbally being able to speak to each other using each other's vocal chords. They are insanely jealous that they cannot do this for themselves however their Hierarchy know of our abilities and to stop us pronouncing this to the world have now forced the 4 to keep

Louise locked up continuously in her flat. She is not allowed to leave her flat at all.

She has no toiletries, FOOD, WATER, she has no way of even wiping her posterior after doing her ablutions, she is not even allowed to wash her bottom after, she is not allowed to bathe regularly or even as much as brush her teeth. WHY we both asked, this is in their eyes because of their torture methods and as they try to belittle her on every occasion they can works out to be every day.

Their hierarchy provide food every day for the 4 as in a cooked meal but leave Louise with nothing and this has been the case for over 6 months to date, that includes water due to the fact like me we don't drink tap water and Louise would prefer not to drink tap water under any circumstance, God has somehow provided a way for the food I eat to give her sustenance also the water I drink hydrates her as I drink bottled water with dilute juice, so far in that, we are lucky.

CHAPTER 4

PROMISES

The 4. 2 black male one with big hair, short, slim build very dark skin (this is the one that rapped his daughter and his wife) and the other approximately 5 foot 4 being the tallest out of the 4 thinking he is tall is very skinny lighter completion , shorter hair. 2 white one formally ginger although it is more grey than ginger now is quite stout along with the person allegedly in charge of the other 3 who had dark brown hair it is more grey than brown now is again stout and short both no more than 5 foot 2. They all pose about in black leather coats aiding them to conceal their weapons

They have continuously promised to allow Louise to leave so she can come to live with me without malice; this has never materialized as they break their promises every day. They love to make bets with her and when they lose the bet, never honour the bet, one of the reasons she is still there.

They have promised to come and attack me be it in my house or out of my own place due to the fact that I should have any weapons on my person.

I explained this to the police but after having told them that Louise was an ex girlfriend of mine, I found out due to a friend and the police it is not her (my ex) that is under duress of which I apologise to her and all her family for having put her through this but it would make no difference as they see me as insane with my findings but Louise was forced to lie and say she was my ex girlfriend and I believed her but as the 4 forced her to lie it is something I have to live with as she does but as we have established who she is that is in the past, they have forced Louise to do many things she is ashamed of but that is something we both have to live with considering this lie went on for nearly 14 years, I have forgiven her but don't think my ex or her family will ever forgive me on that score.

The 4's employers have promised to help get rid of me so they can abscond with Louise when they get the opportunity but getting rid of me has been left in the 4's hands, I promise to make it as difficult as possible, also if I get the opportunity I will help get Louise some form of retribution.

If Louise gives me her real name or her address she has been promised they will KILL her due to the fact they do not want to appear in court for their crimes, now as this is already an impossible situation because without an address or real name I cannot get any help from the police at all, now I will say what I know, she lives in the Brent area of London, 200 yards from a co-op which is on a corner of her estate. The people who work in said co-op know of the 5 going there on a regular weekly basis up until 6 months ago, they know they wear long leather coats as Louise has had to wear one as well! They wanted her to be one of their devils worshiping gang, as she said no they have administered more and different torture techniques but she will prevail due to the fact she is a strong worshipping Christian and a Rasta as I am. She is white make no mistake judgement as god says is his she is a strong believer.

The 4 have promised that if Louise comes to live with me, they are coming to move in with us both, this is unacceptable.

CHAPTER 5

VISION

God has also equipped both me & Louise differently; she has remote vision which is being able to view nearly everything that I see in layman's terms.

She can see everything that comes through my eyes strange as it may seem but so can the 4 now after having raped her; she isn't able to trust anyone because of this. This is an impossible situation because when the 4 are near her they have remote vision too, that is the reason they won't allow her to be by herself or with me. When the distance is increased they will not be able to have any form of E.S.P. Which they are very worried about, they have lied to their employers saying they did not need Louise to be able to perform the tasks we do and having lied are using her as a crux.

The remote vision is on top of her own vision but she manages both quite easily i.e. she does not get confused when she is viewing my end as I live approximately 160 miles from her, I do not have remote vision so while she is using remote vision the 4 regard themselves as special. They are using her in many different ways. Of which I shall explain throughout.

They feel it's to do with the saliva or body fluids that they have taken from her, either way, they have been stolen and due to the nature of this sorry episode they are accountable by new laws that have to be passed when this story comes to fruition.

They have used her vision to keep tabs on me so to speak by ordering her to tell them what I am doing basically as it is not a clear vision they or she receives it is basically a ghostly vision but can be interpreted through her own abilities, not theirs.

They have threatened her and humiliated her for this reason and more along with the torture of burning her, with hot boiling hot water, their torches and used cold water pouring on her, they have used all of their weapons on her sometimes all at the same time other times all using the same weapon on different places of the body.

One holds onto her breast all day and all night, another has cut all of her trousers and sticks his finger up her bottom, while another tries to keep and does putting his fingers up her vagina, this happens every day and night and has been going on from since they have raped her, i.e. for over 15 years. This is pure humiliation as she has said to them countless times she doesn't want this type of treatment, they also have no reason for putting her through this type of treatment.

If she gives me her name or address they have threatened to kill her on the spot or I would already have given more information to the police, the information I have given already is quite substantial however they do not believe a word I have told them it all is in my head according to them.

CHAPTER 6

HEARING

The sense of hearing is acute due to the fact that we both can hear what each other's situation is, i.e. I can hear what is coming through her ears just as she can hear what is coming through mine, the 4 also due to them being in her vicinity also can hear what we hear, i.e. if someone is speaking to me they get the whole conversation which leave it awkward to be able to keep things a secret from these 4 scumbags. This leaves us in a position considering that when they are unsure of what has been said or heard they force Louise to tell them what the sound was, leaving her open to ridicule, and more torture. They have at one stage tried to convince me of Louise speaking by shouting in her ear and spouting their propaganda to influence my decision on some of the foolish things that have been said over the years, luckily this did not work and Louise and I maintain a strict regime where she tells me the truth as to what was said and what sounds I have heard from her end. This is difficult due to the nature of the 4 as they enjoy lying to the point they do this every day and as I said previously, promise her every day that they will allow her to leave under her own steam, this they haven't done just lied about the fact that they would allow her.

I am a DJ/MC and music producer, they have as said audio of what I'm doing here in my own house, they there employers have rigged illegally equipment through our computers, laptops and Macintosh computers ways of monitoring us visually as well as through audio, this is a constant 24 hourly thing which is totally against my wishes, something else that the police ignore, I am being monitored from London and from Lincoln, their employers do not just work from London but have become my stalker's, most of the houses/flats that I have lived in and apartments in Tenerife they have managed to influence my neighbours and found a way to be close enough to be heard by me slagging me off, they have used their equipment to forcefully interrupt my internet connection and have cloned my computers so they have every program, sound and they follow every process I use on my computers, i.e. when I am recording a tune they can follow how, when and what I put into a tune, all of this being illegal they are not doing this in front of me they are doing all of this behind my back however, Louise has the same setup in her flat, she can also monitor what I do on my computers, she also has a video link where she can see my face while I'm at my computer proving there is more than one audio/visual link which I have not agreed to.

This has enabled us to prove that this is more than just a little stalking, this is a very big thing that is going on here which everybody I have spoken to say's it is in my head. The employers of the 4 have more than one form of monitoring they do monitor allegedly not just me, but my family and friends in their own places, they have stolen my contact lists, they have also invaded more than my privacy by listening into my telephone calls, followed me to various places and sounded an alarm to allow their minions to know when I arrived at certain places all over the country even when I went abroad this happened, now this is not a paranoid man speaking this is on evidence of what I have been putting up with over the years due to jealousies and due to the fact of them being devil worshippers and us not wanting to join their disgusting organization. They know of the E.S.P. but have found a way of earning money and I mean lots of money from keeping this a secret. They already are millionaires and don't care to tell people how they make their money!

CHAPTER 7

TASTE

*A*s explained previously Louise has not ate for over 6 months now or drank, due to being confined to her flat although the employers of the 4 feed the 4 regularly, the only way she has managed to stay alive is due to what I eat which God has managed somehow to help her get sustenance from the food I eat. She can taste the food as I can taste what she eats although she is not eating now, when she does I can taste what is passing through her taste buds as she can what is passing through mine, how? We don't know but God somehow has equipped us with each other's senses. This has generated a whole heap of jealousy within the 4 also the people that have employed the 4.

The 4 also can taste what I eat as well which has encouraged them to eat faeces hoping that I could taste what they put in their mouths, suck on each other's penises without having washed them for over 15 years, the smell is horrendous but they are hoping by committing their gay acts that this will make me ill as well as Louise. They lick each other's anuses, fingers after they have been up their anuses and continue looking for new forms of disgust to try and make us ill. Being Christian we do not agree with same sex, sex and their gay goings on are a disgrace to both heterosexual and gay's alike, they are outrageously disgraceful but still want to stay in the closet although they commit these acts in front of Louise. They have also tried to get her to join in with them which she will not allow.

They get frustrated now because they have all 4 become impotent but continuously try to raise a hard on which at the moment they have not been able to manage, which luckily stops the rape being a regular thing. They try to simulate raping each other when they have gay sex. We choose not to discuss this too much as they are monitoring me while I write this and I do not want to encourage anything more along those lines they are freaks that sponge up all the information I have put into words. They are very pleased with themselves having some of the abilities that we have, but as we have already proven, they will not have these abilities when they are not in the vicinity of Louise so, they hold her against her own will in her flat not allowing any form of contact with the outside world. This is wrong, they prefer including their employers to keep this a secret.

There is much, much, more we or I as I am writing this would need to say regarding taste but due to the nature of our problems I choose not to at this moment in time but will add to this in book 2.

CHAPTER 8

THE EVIL

The injuries Louise has sustained over the period of time is unheard of, she has cuts every place on her body, that I can recognise without having ever met her. During this period she has sustained injuries in places internally as well as externally now, these injuries have all been cause by the 4 and they have continuously poured toilet water, wiped faeces as I've mentioned on the wounded areas, thrown petrol, burned her with their torches to try and get septicaemia to set in and kill her on the quiet so the blame is not on the injuries but just the time the injuries have been there. This is abominable as are the 4. The evil is all around us but most specifically in our lives due to their employers and the 4.

The employers although they monitor everything that happens in her 2 bedroom flat have condoned what has been going on over the years because she Louise will not waver in her strict Christian upbringing as they have tried to convert her into a devil worshipper, she will not allow this to happen so they have aided the 4 in providing them with a cooked meal every day, provided the 4 with their weapons. These are to cause as much injury to Louise as possible also to continue with the mêlée and try to commit these acts with me once Louise is dead. Or before as they want her to come to where I reside and use her as a negotiating factor to sway my decision in protecting myself from the evil that the 4 transmit.

They continuously squeeze her left breast mainly sometimes her right breast after having stabbed, cut and stabbed through mainly her left breast, this is mainly the one of the 4 that has already raped his child and his wife in Solihull in Manchester his boyfriend tries to copy what this lowlife does with her other breast unless the left breast has been left alone for a minute he continues on the same breast to administer as much pain as possible and to humiliate her.

All 4 when they get the opportunity stick their fingers up her vagina and simulate sexual acts by moving their fingers back and forth. They use their knives in the same way, this is when she is stood up or sitting down due to them having cut the crutch area of most of her clothes to aid easy access. These are a constant day and night thing for them .One of the four insists on sticking his fingers up her bottom, this again is a constant, i.e. every time she goes to the toilet, when she is in bed, awake or asleep, when she is stood up static or walking again to humiliate her and to try and get turned on ready to start raping her again.

They supposedly have one that is in charge of the 4, he stays in a position that had to be pointed out, underneath her computer table, where he is constantly, that way he knows when at some stage of the day or night he will have Louise in front of him, he also stabs her continuously in the legs, stomach, arms, feet, toes and vagina. I said earlier that they had took the hard part out of the back of the chair but they have also took that out of the seat of the chair which enables them to stab her constantly in the bottom and sometimes vagina from underneath the chair. There are bigger holes from before when they used to rape her in that position while being forced to stay in the chair. There are also holes in the settee back and the seat of the settee which they use to stab and cut her while she was sat down; they have also used bigger holes that they have made to rape her previously. The bed also has the same format and they have used the bed to commit the same acts, although they now are impotent these all happened and we both are hoping they will not get away with it!

During the night when one of them attempts to put his fingers up her bottom he has his hand behind her back which is causing a problem with her back, this is how regular he does this and this is every night. They all apart from their boss sleep in her bed with her although they do not sleep much due to their cocaine habits, they have enough cocaine to last the 4 at least 7 years which is a copious amount as anyone would agree but this was also provided by their employers, imagine the type of people we are faced to deal with although Louise or I will not accept any deal they have to offer.

Approximately 7 years ago, their employers had a following of about 2000 people who all worshipped the devil, another reason why Louise has been in turmoil and worried for my health as well as her own when or if she finally gets out of this horrible situation. They rape children in front of their minion's, male & female have also been put through this situation in front of their followers. Some have been stabbed, cut, also killed in front of their followers, this is fact that Louise has pointed out to me although I have not seen this myself I do believe her as she was put in front of these people and cut stabbed and raped in front of their followers, the female, male and bodyguard who run the sect have raped her in front of them already and this is previous to her teaming up with the 4 who are part of the followers who worship the devil and their employers.

The 4 were at these evil events and this has encouraged them to start their war on Louise ever since.

Now teaming up with the 4 does not mean she allowed their company she was forced into it, she was out one day and returned to her flat to find the 4 inside, all her sharp knives removed from her kitchen and was told they are all in the second bedroom, so she could not protect herself, all heavy objects also have been removed to the second bedroom so she cannot harm them, all sharp objects also. One of the 4 hold her keys as said debit card and purse, which he is holding onto and not allowing her to use, along with her mobile telephone which she hasn't seen for years.

They open her letters, she doesn't get a chance to see them and as most of the bills are paid on direct debit she has no way of letting the authorities know and due to the fact that the landlords are the employers of the 4 the rent is paid directly to them not allowing anybody to find out the problems Louise is facing. She is no longer on the electoral role as they will not allow her to go and vote, she can no longer leave to go to the bank, fetch toiletries or food & water!

They are trying to command her life and that includes everything she does, including what channels she should watch on the TV, when she should bath (without soap or any other form of bath aid) she has to bath with 3 of the 4 in the bathroom, they comment when she gets undressed, cut and stab her before during and after, soon as she's finished in the bath they daub faeces on her even before she has dried herself. She has to hide her hair-band before she goes in the bath or they will steal it from her, she also has to wear glasses but they have been stolen already so she now does not wear glasses. They are always on her case to humiliate and deflate her ego due to them having to bigger ego.

They as we do physcokenisis force her to continually speak in E.S.P. which is to make me speak while not allowing her to speak normally using her usual form of natural speaking, this way they infuriate me all the time because they are trying to make people think I have or am going mad, this is not the case but by disallowing Louise to speak as normal means I have to speak as well as her which is accumulating money for their employers (explanation to be given in book 2) they really are a disgusting breed and need to be in prison now! This doesn't end, they don't allow us to communicate for long periods of time without threatening her with death unless she repeats something of what they are saying, i.e. she has to repeat what they say like a parrot and they most of the time act like her or me! This again is an impossible situation as they cannot do telepathy or physcokenisis but have told their employers that they can, they use her to repeat so people connected to their employers believe they can.

When asked why they are stabbing Louise constantly, they cannot justify a reason for doing this, they make up reasons now for stabbing and cutting her that are so wayward they will be laughed out of court however this is not a laughing matter.

When we are indoors they constantly chloroform her forcing her to sleep at inopportune moments and making sure we don't sleep at the usual times for sleeping, normally the night time so the book is left unwritten, we are not allowing this to be the case and will continue writing the book until it is finished, this book has to be in the public domain to get something done about this sorry state of affairs and very soon.

The main reason as we, Louise and I is that they are trying to administer pain and suffering to me but don't have the bottle to try and do these things to me to my face because I will protect myself at all times and retaliate, they know of this and have taken the cowards way by increasing the anti on Louise. She is constantly under threat of death and is constantly getting stabbed and cut by these heathens again and impossible situation, this is from morning through the night and during the periods we sleep, she gets burned to the point her body is blistered, cut and stabbed so she is constantly bleeding and this is something the 4 put down as normal behaviour, as I see it this is unacceptable behaviour and something has to be done now!

They are trying to kill her on the quiet as said but are in need of her services in E.S.P. they cannot function without have believed they are doing E.S.P. they are so high on cocaine they believe its them where it comes from and in any case what reason is there to treat Louise in this way.… . none.

We are now at the point where God has not let us down but the world has in that this secret is ongoing and has to be unravelled this instant we both Louise and I do not intend to carry on like this as if it's some type of joke, it is no joke to be continuously tortured blaspheming as they are calling God for having know of our talents having stolen someone that does not belong or want to be part of their devil worshipping sect, please get something done about this situation. Remember she lives 200 yards from a co-op with the co-op being on the corner, the staff will recognize 5 people in long leather coats 1 female 4 male 2 black 2 white, she lives in the Brent area of London, if the 4 male have spoken they will have a Manchester accent, not a London accent, the female (Louise would) There are words to describe how we are both feeling but they will be in book 2, let's get something done about this NOW!!!!